Cries from the heart: An anthology of poems from an adoptee

Danielle Bolduc

BookLeaf Publishing

India | USA | UK

Presentation by *BookLeaf Publishing*

Web: www.bookleafpub.com

E-mail: info@bookleafpub.com

ISBN: 9789360941154

First edition 2024

DEDICATION

To my parents and grandparents who have shown me what love is but also whose love knows no bounds. They have paved the path of my journey with their unconditional support through life's storms.

To my extended family, whose embrace spans continents– your love for me is deeply acknowledged and appreciated and I can't wait to get to know you all.

PREFACE

In the tapestry of my life, woven with the threads of adoption, family is both a constellation of love and a mosaic of questions. It is within the embrace of my family that I first learned the language of belonging, where their love became the foundation upon which my identity took root and blossomed. I talk about the dreams that beckon me to seek out the untold chapters of my father's family. Yet, alongside the warmth of familial bonds, there exists a whispered longing, a yearning to unearth the hidden chapters of my ancestry, to traverse the uncharted terrain of my birth family's history.

This anthology is a testament to the many experiences that have shaped my journey as an adoptee – from the tender moments of childhood innocence to the complexities of adulthood. It is a collection born of introspection, resilience, and the unwavering pursuit of truth and understanding.

At its heart lies a poem, penned in the wake of my grandmother's passing, a poignant tribute to the love, loss and the eternal bond of family that reverberate within me.

As I traverse the landscape of memory, I am reminded of the fragmented pieces of my past – the siblings I have yet to meet, the nieces and nephews whom I long to hear. Each poem within these pages is a testament to the numerous emotions that accompany the journey of reunion, reconciliation, and forgiveness.

In the crucible of my existence, I have grappled with the complexities of identity, wrestled with the shadows of abandonment, and navigated the tumultuous waters of self-discovery. From the tumultuous beginnings marked by the scars of maternal rejection to the tender embrace of my family, each verse bears witness to the resilience of the human spirit and the enduring power of love.

As I trace the contours of my narrative, I am confronted by the echoes of my past – the whispered secrets of ancestry, the ache of separation, and the unspoken questions that linger in the depths of my soul. Yet, amidst the shadows, there exists a glimmer of hope – a beacon of resilience that guides me forward, illuminating the path toward healing.

Within these pages, you will find the echoes of my journey – the tears shed in moments of solitude, the laughter shared in moments of joy, and the unspoken truths that resonate within the chambers of the heart.

I have also added two poems that I wrote during my youth when I was 12 and 14 years old. These poems are special because 'Save the Planet' was chosen to be published in the Young Writers anthology in 2009. The second poem 'Remembering Hana' is special as well because I wrote it for a poetry competition I participated in at my school. The story behind it is very special as it's the story of a young girl who died during the Holocaust.

It is my hope that these verses will serve as a source of solace, empathy, and understanding for those who navigate the labyrinth of adoption – a reminder that within the depths of our shared experiences lies the power to heal, to forgive, and to embrace the fullness of our identities. With gratitude and humility, I offer this anthology as a testament to the resilience, the courage, and the unwavering spirit of the adoptee.

Warmly, Danielle Bolduc

My family

In an international tapestry I'm woven
An adoptee upbringing, unique and rare
Born in London, where my roots were sown
But my heritage spreads beyond that nest
Raised in a family of cultures diverse
With roots in London where the story starts
And Italian heritage, a blessing to traverse

My mother, a daughter of Italy's land
A London-born beauty with Italian grace
Her parent's heritage, a story in itself
Weaving culture and love in every embrace
Yet her heart whispered in Neapolitan's tone
Learning the language from neighbours so kind
Her Italian roots, a love deeply sown

My father, a French Canadian man
Together our paths intertwined and entwined
With his own story, a chapter untold
Attending a boys' catholic boarding school
Where faith and knowledge forever aligned

Every Friday, his father's smile would appear
To pick him up, not a visit missed
Opposite the collège, the Basilica stood
A symbol of devotion, forever filled

Surrounded by love, a fortunate life

With Italian grandparents, I was raised
In a Catholic family, my spirit was praised
My upbringing, a tapestry of love
With parents and Italian grandparents dear
Attending the best schools, blessed from above
A life filled with love and guidance

Raised in a Catholic family's embrace
Two sacraments, deeply ingrained
Baptism's waters, first holy communion's grace
Where faith and knowledge forever aligned
But confirmation, I couldn't partake
Though incomplete, my sacramental journey
In the end, it's not the rituals we attain,
But the love we share, and the lessons we gain
My family, a beacon of love and support

Evening masses with my grandmother, I'd share
The church, a sanctuary of solace and peace
The stained glass windows, a masterpiece
divine,
The scent of church fills the air
Burning candles, incense rising with care
In those moments, love hung in the air
A bond with the Divine, a sweat release

Yet, part of me yearns for the unknown

My father's sisters, half a family unseen
Dreaming of Canada, a place to be shown
Hoping my dream of reunion to be true

A distant land beckons, Canada's embrace
Where my aunt resides, an awaited delight
To bridge the gap, this longing I'll chase
Embrace the bond, one that is new

Trips to Italy, where my parent's work thrived
A land of beauty and delight
Residing by the sea, a luxury untold
Indulging in Mediterranean flavours, a feast for
the sole
A life enriched, a story yet to unfold

From my grandmother's lips, Italian would flow
Learning the language and dialect, a bond to last
Every word, a lesson, a language so grand
Her wisdom and love, a cherished grace

Fortunate, yes, my life has been blessed
With a tapestry woven from love's embrace
A blend of cultures, a life filled with grace
With love and heritage, my heart will sway
Grateful for the journey that has made me whole
The story unfolds of an adoptee's upbringing, so
rare
A fortunate life, beyond compare

Nonna Adalgisa

From a southern Italian village that's where you came
Calabritto was its name
With only primary school education in hand
But with your determination, you couldn't withstand
With your husband my dear grandfather Lorenzo
an adventure was to begin

1952 was the year, they ventured for London's embrace with hope
London the city of dreams
The first to do such a thing
From a village to a city
Calabritto to London you came

From Mussolini to Churchill and the Queen
Creating a new home, a foreign land to embrace
To a new home, a coronation had started
A foreign tongue they did not comprehend, they faced their fears
From your father in law you learnt the basics
Such as 'A pound of potatoes please'
Your knowledge would ascend in time

Seamstress was your trade, a talent so rare
Not surprising, as a family of sarti (tailors) you
share
Creating garments with skill and precision
From a lineage of tailors producing uniforms for
the military
Talents intertwined
Phones would ring, seeking my grandmother's
flair
From Mary Quant, to Beta, to Bonpoint, to
David Charles to name just a few

My grandfather a man so strong, a prisoner of
war based in Kenya
Malaria invading his body
How different life's tapestry would be
We might not have got to experience, you as
husband, father or grandfather
Cobbler was my grandfather's trade, for Lilley
and skinner was it's name
Crafting shoes with love
Their expertise renowned
Like blessings from above

From Islington, to Kingsland to Stamford hill
Your heart was always full of kindness and
generosity
Opening your doors to kin in need

Brothers, sisters, niece or nephews, their
families indeed
Under your roof, they found comfort, shelter and
care
A testament to your kindness, beyond compare
From her compassionate heart her generosity
flowing knew no bounds, she'd always be there

In later years, as time went by
Everyday visiting your sister Maria, a routine for
her soul
Through rain and storm, she'd make her way
Undeterred by the weather, come what may
Her dedication would show
Drenched but undiscouraged
Her devotion held strong
A love unbreakable

As your granddaughter you welcomed me with
open arms
A testament to your loving charms
As a young child in a foreign land
You embraced me, held my hand
With you, I said my first few words
'On the bus' were the words that I spoke
Memories of bringing me to church
Hand in hand, we walked the path
Memories of you bringing and picking me up
from school

A constant presence in my life
From you I learnt your mother tongue but also
the dialect of Calabritto
A thing my family finds so rare

Such an incredible woman, why did you have to
go
As a family we now mourn our loss and your
absence from us all
We shed tears that she is gone, surreal that she's
not here
Our hearts empty since we can't see her
But at the same time blessed for the love and
experience we shared

In the house where memories reside
I stand alone
A tender bond we shared
But now we're left in silent despair
Missing your voice, so sweet and kind
And your presence, forever entwined
In this empty house, echoes remain
Whispering tales of love's refrain

Dear grandmother, so active and involved
Your caring touch, I now long to behold
You were there, always near

But now, a shock, a sudden blow
You left this world, a place I still know
The void you've left, impossible to fill
A heartache that time can never heal

Yet, I find solace in the memories we shared
In the love we had, the moments we cared
Though you're gone, your spirit remains
In every heartbeat, in life's refrains

So, as I stand here, in this empty space
I honour you with love and grace
For you were more than a grandmother to me
You were a guiding light, eternally free

65 years at the grand Stamford Hill house
Memories engrained in the walls
From the times of my mother's childhood and
youth
To more recent times to living under your roof

My grandparent's legacy, a testament so grand
Defying limitations, with love in their hands
My dear grandparents, your journey so grand
From a village in Italy to a foreign land
With limited education you defied the odds
Creating a legacy, in the face of all unknowns
Your strength and resilience, forever admired
Your love and compassion, forever inspired

Through stories, your spirit thrives
In my heart, your legacy forever survives

Freedom

In the quiet corners of my heart, a shift occurs
As an adoptee now, I have found freedom
No longer shackled by the weight of anger
towards birth parents who once seemed a
mystery

I am free now, free to embrace my story
To unravel the threads of my birth family's
history
No hiding behind walls of resentment
But open, willing to see the truth with clarity

The past no longer holds me captive
I walk forward with a lighter step
Embracing the complexities of my identity
With a new sense of peace and acceptance

There is still some pain, lingering in the corners
But my outlook has shifted, transformed

No longer do I carry anger or sadness
Instead, I embrace a new way of being
I navigate life with a belief of forgiveness
Not as a gift to my birth parents, but as a gift to
myself

Forgiveness is the key to my liberation
I release the chains that bind me to the past
I let go of the part of me that holds onto hurt
No longer a prisoner, I am free to soar

In this newfound freedom, I find strength
To navigate the twists and turns of my journey
Embracing both my past and present
With a heart open to the endless possibilities of
the future

My brothers whom I've never met

I've never met you but the love I have for you is
huge
I will patiently wait until I get the news that you
want to see me too
When I eventually see you I will run to you and
hug you both tight

I've tried so hard to know something about you -
even a minute detail of what you look like
Nothing out there seems to work, am I just
unlucky I ask myself
All I know that you my brothers are out there
somewhere

I dream of the day that I will see both of your
faces and I will cry with delight
You will no longer be boys but young men
instead
I just hope the day will come when you both
reach 18
Even though we have never met, I miss you both
I've often wondered if you know that I exist

In summer I found out some very sad news

Your adoptive mother had passed away
What a shock that was to hear
What's happened to you now, orphans that you
are

I love you both so much
Hopefully my dream will come true sometime
very soon
I will keep smiling for you both, my brothers
I will keep dreaming as I've done for years,
that's what keeps me going
With love, your sister Danielle

The one and only reunion

In shadows of my past, a tale unfolds
As an adoptee, my journey unfolds
No contact I will allow, no ties to bind
For danger awaits, within my birth's kin

Their words, like daggers, pierce my soul
Spiteful, aggressive, throwing accusations, they
take their toll
Leaving scars that refuse to console
And so, I must tread with caution and care
For their presence brings suffering, I cannot bear

Though blood may bind, it does not define
The essence of family, a love so divine
For in my heart, I've found solace and peace
In the arms of those who've made pain cease

Family who've become my chosen kin
Their acceptance, a balm that lies deep within
They understand the ache, the yearning I bear
Without judgment, they're always there

No, I cannot risk my well-being's troubles
To invite toxicity into my life's light
For my happiness thrives in a different sphere

Where love and compassion will always appear
So I'll embrace the freedom that comes with
release
From the toxicity that brings me no peace
And forge ahead, with courage in my stride
As an adoptee, finding joy on this ride

I walk this path, with courage and might
For my journey's worth, I shall fight
As an adoptee, I forge my own way
In the absence of birth's kin, I find my place to
stay

Ancestry

In the depths of a soul, an adoptee's yearning
A search for roots, a quest for belonging
With whispered hopes and ancestral dreams
She delves into the past, the unseen

From 1730, her paternal side unfurls
A family tree, branches reaching the world
Names etched in history, stories untold
Echoes of heritage, secrets unfold

And on her maternal side, from 1788
A tapestry woven, memories revived
Ancestors scattered across oceans wide
To lands of New Zealand and Australia's pride

Through faded photographs, she sees their faces
Eyes in far-off places
Census documents, like whispers in the wind
They tell a tale of kinship, where her heart began

A cousin in New Zealand, a bridge to the past
A connection found, will that last
They build a bridge across the years

She yearns for more, to know her birth's truth

Yet circumstances bind her, a bittersweet truth
But within these ancestral ties, she finds her
grace
A sense of pride, a belonging in this space

Ancestry tells her that English roots run deep
Jewish, Irish and Scottish too
Traces intertwine
Swedish, Danish blend
A tapestry of heritage
Stories yet untold

French elegance shines
Germanic echoes resound
Ancestral whispers
In blood's legacy
A patchwork of many lands
She finds her true self

For blood may not bind, but love transcends
And in her heart, a family she amends
With each discovery, a new chapter penned
A legacy of strength, her spirit ascends

Through the shadows of the past she strides
Embracing her roots, with unwavering pride
An adoptee's journey, a story to be told
A testament to resilience, a spirit bold
In the depths of her soul, a fire ignites

A search for self, a beacon of light
She may never know her birth parents' embrace
But she's found her belonging, in this ancestral
chase

Roots

Roots intertwine people but some people take
their roots for granted
Not realizing that without them we are
transplanted
I am a tree but where are my roots
I'm reaching for the stars
But my broken heart yearns for the deep soil

Without my roots 'who am I then'?
I am searching for the secrets of my past
Looking for the faces who are strangers
Stories that are untold and forever unknown
Questioning myself relentlessly with the same
question I wonder

Who am I, I ask myself again and again
Puzzles yet to be complete
We stand in between two worlds
One in the past and one in the present
A door between two hearts
Amidst the secrets a heritage unknown
Still searching from time to time for my old
roots

Damaged hearts will unite, will it bring some
attributes
I bloom where I am replanted not where I was
originally planted
Sewn together by the two families
One full of love and one which is dysfunctional
and where hatred exists

New history is generated continuously
Bound by invisible ties
With the truth being that true answers derive
from roots
Searching is healthy, it should never give us
illnesses
However roots can affect us from the days in the
womb
If unanswered we will not bloom
I find my strength amidst all of this

Button

In a button, a tale of roots untold
An adoptee's identity takes hold
A surname, a label, a lineage's grace
Contained within this tiny, precious space

A button's surface, a canvas serene
Reflects a journey, a story unseen
A name bestowed, a new chapter begun
Binding the past with threads yet undone

Eyes filled with wonder, searching for a trace
A familial connection, a familiar ace
A button's significance, simple and pure

For in this small object, a name resides
A heritage embraced, no longer hides
An adoptee's identity, forever sealed
Within a button's embrace, their truth revealed

Adoptee's button, surname identity shines
Whispered legacy, unseen thread weaving stories
Roots finding their way
Past and present merge, inheritors bloom
Identity blooms, buttoned name a tender bud

A name like petals, unfolding, revealing the
truth
Strength in belonging

Button's silent voice, echoes of forgotten kin
Miller, Button merge
Names entwined, a fusion of selves
Identity forged, in the fires of dual names
Strength in duality

Leo

In the realm of stars, my spirit roams free
A Leo, bold and fierce, I proudly am
With fiery mane, I walk this mortal plane
Resilient strength, my birthright I attain

Like a lion, I stand tall unyielding
A heart ablaze, passion forever building
Through trials faced, my courage shall not wane
For in my veins, the fire shall remain

A lion's heart beats strong within my chest
Endurance and fortitude, my legacy
Though challenges may rise, I shall not fear
For I am a Leo, shall persevere
In every battle fought, I claim my place

A Leo's strength, a symbol of grace

UK has no support

In this land of swirling mists and ancient tales
Where history weaves its intricate trails
As an adoptee, I ponder with a heavy heart
Why, in the UK, we are set apart

No support for us, the children of adoption
Lost in a system that lacks compassion
In this triad of love, loss and pain
We search for solace but all in vain

For everyone involved, it seems they care
But for us, the forgotten, it's hard to bear
This country, not child-centred at all
Leaves us longing, our hearts torn apart

In other lands, we hear whispers of hope
Where adoptees are embraced, given scope
There, they find comfort, understanding and grace
But here, our tears fall, without a trace

UK, you boast of fairness and might
Yet fail to see our struggles, day and night
Your child-centred approach, a distant dream
As we navigate a system, broken at the seams

But let us not lose hope in this dark hour
For change can come, not now but in the far
future
Let's raise our voices, unite as one

For as an adoptee, I yearn to see
A country that cherishes love and sets us free
Where compassion flows like a gentle breeze
And the adoption triad finds solace with ease

So, let us rally our voices strong
For the rights of adoptees, we shall prolong
In this UK, let child-centricity bloom
Creating a haven, where love can consume

Being adopted

In shadows deep, I wandered all alone
A soul adrift, searching for my own place
But destiny had whispered in the unknown
And led me to a love I can embrace

For in the arms of strangers, I did find
A bond unbroken, woven by pure grace
With tender hearts, they nurture me, so kind
And gave me wings to soar in life's embrace

In the tapestry of life, a thread unknown
A tale of roots unspoken, yet tightly sewn
For I am the child who found love anew
In the gentle embrace of family true

I am the bud that bloomed in new soil
Where love was the sunlight
With every milestone, every precious first
A tapestry woven, a story rehearsed

Yet beneath the surface, questions arise
A longing to know, to seek the skies
The whispers of genes, the echoes of the past
I've come to know the truth within the heart
For love transcends the bloodlines we explore

And family is a tapestry of art

An innocent child, lost in the unknown
Longing for siblings, a bond never sown
But that wish, never came to be
Forever alone, a solitary tree

I am a soul unique and complete
With a heart that beats its own rhythmic beat
For being adopted is not just a name
But a testament to love's transformative flame

In the arms of family, I found my place
A haven of love, a haven of grace
For in this tapestry of life, we all intertwine
Where love knows no boundaries, no defined
line

So let my voice sing, with joy and grace
Of a life embraced, a special place
Adopted, I stand proud and free
A testament to love's unending decree

Mirror

Mirror Mirror on the wall is it possible for
another person to bring me to my misery
Mirror mirror yes I'm able to see how strong this
person resembles me
You are detached from me but is it just me
clinging for closeness which I'm unable to see

I'm trying to figure out how we can prosper
I'm thinking but it's impossible for us to become
a we
All you see in me is I a stranger
You are detached from me

I am looking for acceptance, love, honesty and
welcomeness but none I see
I'm trying to figure out why you sent me away
and abandoned me
What have I done wrong NOTHING

Is this what happens when your children connect
with you in some sort of way
You depart when someone is interested and
wants to get close
I wish this was a dream but unfortunately this is
how reality has treated me

Why were you so cold and distant towards me

Mirror mirror on the wall I didn't know reunion
would treat me like this
All that you have done is brought me to my own
destruction
At the moment I have to weep like a willow tree,
it too feels my inner pain

Now now I have to recover, how long I don't
know
You are now apart from me and not welcome
Now now I see I was blinded from your true
inner self
The time has come to say goodbye and for me to
get you out of my mind
Fair thee well

Adoption is both

I am adopted so that makes me an adoptee
An adoptee means I can be happy, sad, hold
grief and alone
Other emotions exist too, the list goes on

The reality of adoption is that happiness and
sadness coexist
It's not honky dory as the world portrays
At times adoption is like a hole in my heart
where I carry void
But at times I can be very happy and annoyed
Moments exist when I think and miss the people
from my past

Questions pour down like a river but who should
I have asked
A lot of my history is unknown which I call it
mystery
what happened just has to be in the past
Truths in adoptions are rare

There are other days I want to be joyful and
celebrate the family I have
Adoption made my family and that is greatness

However adoption doesn't define me, that's just
one aspect of me

Grief and gratitude can exist simultaneously
Hope and heartache can live in the same space
Joy and sorrow can be both present
Acceptance is key to an adoption story

Some like talking but it's okay to keep your
story inside
Sharing is optional not compulsory, you decide
Adoptees are resilient and strong
We carry a lot of pain and weight
But most of all we can get through this fight

We can be whoever we want to be
We can be doctors, teachers, judges, lawyers,
nurses, social workers, journalists or even pilots
It doesn't matter what you do, happiness is the
key!

Adoption can feel like a dark, heavy
forever-ending storm
But it won't last forever, trust me!
Time is the essence to healing
We need support which is like a needle in a
haystack
Optimism is what I live by and something I can't
take back

There is no doubt that adoption is happy and sad
It's okay to be content and mad
Adoption is full of colours, you could call it a
rainbow
Adoption is green, blue and red!
But one colour could dominate them all, only
you decide what comes ahead
All are perfectly normal

The hole in my heart

The quest is not over only postponed
For I must move on, yet I don't know which
road to turn
I feel I need her by my side
To fill in where the gap lies

I yearn for her yes, but physical contact is too
much for me to handle at the moment
Yet she is my birth mother and the barrier there
lies
She did not bring me up or nurture me to be who
I am today
Yet she does not know nor understand me

There are moments when I'm angry at her for
letting me go
And I having to deal with the roller coaster of
emotions that lies there ahead
Yet at the same time, I think about her though
But at the same time if it wasn't for all of this
my family wouldn't exist
I wouldn't be where I am today, a university
graduate

I used to wish that I would get to know you
better and have a relationship with the birth
mother of mine but for now not today
I have to search for who I truly am and to heal
my inner troubles
The chances are over, you've wasted your
opportunities to get to know who your daughter
is
Time is for me now and for me to live my life
Free from worrying and without my thoughts
revolving around you
That's over and in the past
A new life begins for me now today

My unknown nieces and nephew

In the depths of my heart, a longing resides
An ache that echoes through the unseen tides
For in this vast world, where love intertwines
I am an adoptee, lost in the confines

Never have I seen the eyes so bright
Of nieces and nephews, bathed in pure light
Their laughter, like music, a symphony of joy
Yet, fate has kept me apart

Through the tangled webs of foster care and
kinship care
Their lives unfold, while I am left unaware
In dreams, I imagine their faces so dear
But reality's touch brings a silent tear

How I yearn to hold them close
To witness their growth, their dreams transpose
To be the aunt they've never known
A bond untangled, gently sown

But time slips away, like sand through my grasp
So, I cherish the moments in the photos I have,
however far

In my heart, they dwell, like a distant star

For family is not merely bound by blood
But the love that transcends, like a flood
And though I may never hold them near
I send my love, whispered in every tear

So, let them know, as they journey through life's
maze
That an adoptee's love forever stays
To be reunited, and set their spirits free

A social worker named Samantha

Samantha, social worker kind and true
I met you as an adult, seeking my past
To pick up my file, my story askew
With trepidation, my secrets amassed

But in your presence, a safe space did bloom
A haven for my deep innermost thoughts
With gentle patience, you'd banish my gloom
Listening intently, no matter the knots

Your words like whispers, carried hope's
embrace
Unwavering faith in my journey's unfold
Each session a solace, a saving grace
In your empathy, my spirit consoled
Thank you, for the light you shared
For being the one who truly did care

Social worker, I thank you for the truth
For guiding me when darkness clouded sight
In moments of despair, you helped me through
And taught me strength to face my endless fight

You showed me that the burdens I had borne
Were not my fault
With gentle words, you gave me hope
And from constant fear, my mind was turned
Many would have seen me drown, ignored me
but you were different

I thank you for your positive energy
I thank you for believing in me
And most of all I thank you for giving me my
life back
I wouldn't be where I am today if it weren't for
you
Today I'm no longer that vulnerable person that
you last saw of me
I am where I am today feeling confident with
my dreams fulfilling one step at a time

Your positivity a radiant sun
Shone brightly, breaking through my deepest
gloom
In your presence, my battles had been won
And I emerged with hope, no longer doomed

Few souls can make a difference so profound
But Samantha, your impact will resound
You were inspirational to me and you'll never be
forgotten
Thank you so much Samantha Christodoulou

My file

As an adoptee, I received my file
A five-year wait, anticipation grew
But disappointment within me did reside
For crucial pieces were missing, it's true

But as I delved into those pages of mine
Disappointment filled me, I did not find
Where were the details of my foster care years
Or the reports from my time in the mother and
baby unit

Most of my life, information hidden away
I know it exists, yet it's kept at bay
My older sister, fortunate with her file and the
truth
Why not me? It's unjust, I must pursue

Social services weaving a web of dishonesty
Lies engraved upon the lines incomplete
But I won't surrender, I won't give in
This fight for my past, I am determined to win

Lucky, I sat with a compassionate soul
A social worker, understanding and kind
In time just before the council's cyber attack

Now an excuse, their negligence I find

My story, my records held back
But this is not the whole truth, I firmly believe
In due course, when the moment feels right
The whole truth, I'll continue to pursue

Through the echoes of my past, I'll rise
Unveiling the hidden truths, no more disguise
I'll persist, for my history must bloom

My inner deep pain

In the depths of my soul, a pain resides
Born from a journey I did not choose
As an adoptee, I've faced a tempest's tide
Years spent grappling with a heart bruised

From the moment I sought my roots
Unveiling a tangled web of sorrow
Birth parents, in their pursuits
Greeted me with aggression, no tomorrow

Their welcome was not warm, nor kind
But a storm of hostility and threat
Yet, in my heart, I still yearned to find
A glimmer of love, a hope to be met

But their hearts remained closed
Their embrace withheld, a bitter sting
I navigated a path, burdened and imposed
Seeking solace in the pain it would bring

Years have passed, and I've learned to heal
To forge my own path, my own destiny
The pain, once vulnerable begins to reveal
Strength and resilience, now part of me

For in the midst of darkness, I've found light
In the arms of those who truly care
A family built on love, beyond blood to bear

So I rise above the wounds that bind
Embracing the scars that mark my past
A sense of belonging, I will find
In love's embrace that forever lasts

As an adoptee, I've faced pain
But in its wake, I've discovered my worth
With each passing day, I walk a different path
Embracing love, a treasure uncovered

Subconscious brain

In the depths of mind, where secrets dwell
As an adoptee, we weave a spell
A subconscious brain, forever awake thoughts
flowing freely, for our soul's sake

No pause, no respite they dance and roam
Like rivers wild, they find no home
Whether we want to or not, they persist
An automatic symphony, that can't be dismissed

Whispers of heritage, faint and obscured
Ancestral echoes, forever unheard
Through dreams and visions, they softly seep
In the realm of subconscious, they vigilantly
keep

Like ancient rivers, they cave their way
Leaving imprints, where memories sway
The yearning for roots, a constant refrain
Etched on our souls, a lifelong campaign

As an adoptee, we bear this weight
A symphony of thoughts, in infinite wave
But in our subconscious, we find solace true
A sanctuary of whispers where dreams come
true

Conversations in the dark

In the stillness of the night, I speak
Conversations with myself, profound and deep
As the world sleeps, my mind won't rest
For I am an adoptee, on a unique quest

Through the twists and turns, life has shown
I navigate the unknown, though sometimes alone
Uncertainty looms, tomorrow unclear
But I hold onto strength, banishing the fear

Who am I? A question so grand
Yet within my heart, I firmly stand
For I am not defined by my past alone
But by the resilience, within me that has grown

The echoes of hurt, they haunt my soul
Yet I believe in a future that can make me whole
Will my birth family hurt me again?
A worry that lingers, like a shadowed refrain

But I refuse to let darkness prevail
I won't let my spirit fade
Strong, I rise from my family's foundation
Enduring, adamant, with determination
The story untold, the ending unknown

But I won't be broken, I'll continue to work on
the strength that resides deep within my core
A beacon of hope, forevermore

For in this journey, I have found
A strength that knows no bounds
So I carry on, through life's unknown bend
With the resilience of an adoptee, until the very
end

Recovering

In shadows cast by a past unknown
I am an adoptee, a soul untethered
Seeking solace in the depths of my heart
Where wounds lie dormant, unseen and scarred

It takes time, they say to heal and mend
To find strength to rise and ascend
From the tangled web of my birth family's lore
To embrace the unknown, to search for more

For I am an adoptee, a puzzle yet to complete
Yearning to discover my roots, bittersweet
The echoes of questions, like whispers in the
night
Seeking answers, seeking truth, seeking light

But time is a patient healer, guiding me along
Nudging me forward, helping me grow strong
With each passing day, I learn to let go
To embrace the uncertainty, the ebb and the flow

And as I journey through this intricate dance
I find solace in the beauty of happiness
For in the tapestry of life, I am woven anew

A mosaic of love, of resilience, of something
true
So I let my heart heal, let it mend at its pace
For I am an adoptee, embracing grace
In the arms of a journey, both tender and wild
Finding solace in the love of a chosen child

Support is what I need

Support, all I seek as an adoptee
To navigate the depths of my emotions
To mend the wounds from this reunion journey

In the quiet corners of my soul
Resides a longing, a yearning to be whole
To find solace in the arms of care
To heal the scars that still linger, unfair

For I am an adoptee, a child of two worlds
Tethered to the past, unfolded
The reunion, a tumultuous tide
A rollercoaster of emotions I cannot hide

But in this whirlwind of uncertainty
Support, a lifeline, I plea
A gentle touch, a listening ear
To hold my hand, to calm my fear

To understand the complexities I face
To help me navigate this foreign place
To unravel the layers of this newfound
connection
To heal the wounds with love's affection

For support is the bridge that spans the divide
The foundation on which I confide
In the embrace of understanding hearts
I find solace, where healing starts

So, let empathy be my guiding light
As I traverse this emotional fight
Support, the foundation of my healing path
To mend the wounds, reclaim my worth

For as an adoptee, I seek not pity
But a safe space to unravel, to be strong
To find strength in vulnerability
To heal, to grow, to be truly free

Siblings split up

Lost in a sea of unknown
Adoptee's heart yearns to find
Brothers yet unseen

Whispers of their existence
Echo through the empty night
Longing fills the void

Shared blood, a secret bond
Silent kinship unexplored
Haunting thoughts persist

Mysteries wrapped in shadows
Invisible threads that bind
Yearning to be known

Unspoken stories untold
Memories yet to unfold
Brothers yet unseen

Through the mist of time
Destiny's path intertwines
Fate's embrace awaits

Though time may have kept us apart
Our souls forever connected
Eternal bond formed

Wishing for brothers
Time has slipped away, through my searching
hands
My heart yearns to meet you

When I was in reunion you were young boys
Just eight and ten
It was just a dream

Years have swiftly passed
Efforts to find you, in vein
Hope still flickers on

Where have you been, my dear brothers
I've searched so hard but nothing has come true
yet
But still, my heart echoes your whispered names

Dreaming of the day
Our souls finally unite
Longing to embrace

My dear brothers
In dreams, I see us reunited now
A cherished hope, a wish I can't allow

The best teacher

You were patient and supportive, my guide
Arriving just when I needed your support
Through every challenge, you stood by my side
A beacon of light

Each achievement, you rejoiced and praised
Sharing with the staff, my blossoming bloom
In your eyes, my potential was appraised
Fuelling my dreams, dispelling the gloom

Safe and secure, I confided in you
Revealing the secrets hidden in my heart
Of being adopted, a tale so true
You were the first, the one who played the part

Nominating me for an esteemed award
A teacher acknowledging my success
You saw beyond my flaws, my disguise
Believing in me, you never viewed me any less

You meant the world, a cherished memory
Even when I ventured far from that school
We stayed connected, a bond that's free
You offered your time, a heartfelt embrace

Thank you for being there throughout the years
Though silence lingers, I still hold you dear
Reconnecting with you, my longing sincere

You are one of a kind, a teacher, a mentor so rare
In your presence, I felt seen, heard and cared
Forever grateful for all that you've done
Thank you so much Caroline Stanton

My Birth father

In the depths of my soul, an adoptee's tale
unfolds
A journey entwined with darkness untold
A birth father, a figure of pain and strife
A turbulent experience that shadowed my life

Verbal arrows pierced, emotions ran high
His words, like daggers, cut through the sky
Questioning my existence, my very core
Demanded proof, a DNA test
To see if I was his kin

Comparisons made, to my sisters
I longed to be seen, my own self to appear
But he, blinded by bitterness and disdain

An awful time, a chapter of despair
His cruelty, a burden I was forced to bear
Blaming my silence on my loving kin
Creating a narrative, a twisted din

Yet I stand here today, strong and resolved
For I am not defined by the pain involved
I am more than his doubts, his toxic claim
A survivor, reclaiming my own name

I am a testament to resilience and grace
With a heart that beats, finding its own space
No longer bound to his tormenting gaze
I embrace my truth, in a healing blaze

For I am an adoptee, a warrior of light
Navigating the shadows, reclaiming my right
To be seen, acknowledged and loved for who I
am
A journey of healing, a triumphant time

So I let the past fade, its power undone
For I am rising, like the morning sun
Embracing my worth, my authentic soul
Writing my story, taking back control

Hermander

In shadows cast by truths that time unfolds
An adoptee's journey, tale of the heart
A birth mother's words a story untold

Lost in a cruel web, birth mother's heart cold
Love twisted to hate, dangerous echoes
Dysfunction's haunting whispers, Seven children
scarred
Social workers came, took us away one at a time

At eighteen, I came looking for you, a fifteen
year wait
You weren't interested in me though
How hard was it to love me
It's as simple as do re me and 1,2,3

All I've heard from you and your family is
predictions
"why no boyfriend yet?"
She whispered in my ear, with a heavy sigh
"no children of your own," she would imply
Her longing for grandchildren plain to see

A yearning born from wounds that never healed
Unable to raise her own precious kin

Her vision blurred, her hope forever sealed
A family unsafe, where pain resides within

And so, her fears projected onto me
A future lost, a path I cannot see

Contact stopped, about time, a fresh start
No more cruel torment, negative words left
behind
Adoptee's heart heals
Resilience, strength within
Hope blooms anew, choosing a new path

But in my heart, a strength begins to rise
A flame of hope, a promise yet untold
For through her words may cast a darkened
guise
A truth within my soul begins to unfold

The love I'll nurture, not defined by blood
A family forged by bonds that cannot break
In safety, warmth is where there is love

For I have learned, through struggles I have
faced
That safety lies in choices we make
To break the cycle, find a better place
To shield our children from the shadow we bear

So, dear birth mother, with a heavy heart
Your doubts and fears, I'll gently lay to rest
For in my journey, I shall play my part
To create a haven where all hearts are blessed

No matter what the future may unveil
I'll lead with love

My Older Sister

In the depths of silence, a tale unfolds
A sister lost, a bond shattered at four
Their paths diverged, never to meet anymore

At a contact centre, Bluewater that we saw each
other
The last glimpse of your face, embedded in my
heart

Years passed swiftly, like whispers in the breeze
Yet the longing lingered, a constant unease
life's complexities veiled my sister's way
A maze of shadows, no light to guide her day

Choices were made, a distance grew wide
And the adoptee's heart, it silently cried
She yearned for a connection, a reunion of souls

The years turned into memories, fading and grey
like fragments of dreams, slipping away
The adoptee pondered, with a heavy heart
should she reach out

At eighteen social media's embrace
A glimmer of hope, a connection it seemed
Yet disappointment soon took its rightful place

But life's tangled threads cannot be easily
undone
And the complexities woven, cannot be outrun
For sometimes, love must take a different course
A painful decision, a bittersweet remorse

Unhealthy lifestyle, aggression abound
Yet disappointment awaited, a bitter sting
Unveiling the painful truth
Unhealthy choices, a lifestyle unkind
Aggressive behaviour, a turbulent find
To meet you now, not the right time I've found

With a heavy heart, I made a choice
Not out of spite, but a longing for calmness
For my sister, dear, I truly care

For you have lost your children, two in all
Through foster care, and kinship care, they roam
The weight of this burden, it does befall
A life merged by pain, a sorrowful tune
A cycle that could not be broken

And so, my sister, though my heart does yearn
To bridge the gap, to heal the wounds of past

Your journey, it must take a different turn
A choice to wait, to let the storm recast

For now, the time is not yet on our side
And my family supports the path I've chosen
To protect my spirit, my heart divide
Until the day when healing's breeze will blow

As an adoptee, I hold you dear
But for now, distance keeps our love sincere

Remembering Hana

I remember my sister; very well.
Her blonde hair, her blue eyes,
Her pretty round face.
I remember playing together,
In the snow, in 1938.
She was my very strong sister.
We watched her, every year, skate
In her special red outfit.
We skied together and laughed
And stood side by side when times were hard

Thinking of her makes me sad.
But the memories make me glad.

I have no mother nor father now.
I wonder … How?
What about my sister Hana?
One day, I had bad news;
Hana's friend told me, confused:
"Hana was sent to Auschwitz.
She died the same day.
In a gas chamber.
I'm sorry, George. Hana's dead."
For me, that was the end.

Thinking of her makes me sad.
But the memories make me glad.

Then from Tokyo a letter came.
'On the suitcase was her name ...'
I went to see it; I was moved.
That she existed the suitcase proved.
Facing a difficult situation,
She placed the suitcase on the platform.
The last thing she held.
I stood looking at it, speechless.
This is all that was left of her.

The memories make me glad,
Though thinking of her makes me sad.

This poem was inspired by the book, 'Hana's
suitcase'
Based on the life of Hanička Bradyová

Save the Planet

Close the curtains, switch off the lights
We need to save the planet
Travel around using a bike
Not the time for using cars
The planet is short of petrol
Don't waste paper otherwise there will be hardly
any trees in the rainforest
And we won't be able to breathe
The ice caps are melting
And the animals are losing their habitats
The climate is changing
And the seasons don't really exist anymore
Recycle everything
Don't be lazy and not bother
If not, the planet will die

The piano

In the hallway of my grandparents' house
An old piano sits silently
It's make is L. G Lyon from no later than 1895
Its keys untouched, its melody hushed
A memory of lessons once renowned

I started piano lessons at age eight
With a Russian teacher who saw potential in me
Piano melodies, a sweet breeze
But soon I turned to strings, a violoncello's call
The music drew me in, a different sound
A new love that captured my heart
And the piano faded into the background

Yet when I see the old piano in the hallway
I feel a tug at my heartstrings
A longing for music that once flowed through
my small fingers
Though unplayed, it holds a place in my heart
The piano's songs will linger evermore
A symbol of my musical journey
Through the keys of an instrument that still
whispers to me

From foster care to a new home

In innocence we arrived, both young and small
My sister and I, to a world unknown
Through foster care's uncertain, troubled hall
To a home where seeds of abuse were sown

Our hearts burdened by a past unseen
By the lady we called Granny Mary
Her son beside her, an abusive strife
But within those walls, danger lingered there
A place where darkness cast it's bitter spell
I, the youngest shielded from the knife
But my sister, not so fortunate
Our innocence shattered, hidden from sight

Yet hope emerged, a flicker in the dark
The foster carer saw potential, said I was bright
University material were her words
Yet communication became a fight day and night
A future bright, a story yet to unfold

The foster family feared my voice
What truths I might reveal, too much to bear
So they did their utmost to silence me, to no
avail

For truth and resilience, I would not spare

In a sailor outfit, I arrived at three
Too big for my small, fragile frame to bear
A memory now, hanging in the wardrobe
A symbol of a time burdened with despair
With my sister, near six by my side

With me came a bear, nameless, unknown and
lost
But my mother named him Sammy forever more
Through journeys and losses, he's always shown
A fortunate bear, through life's endeavours
Faithful companion always
Through travels and tears

But my sister, she could not stay with me
For danger loomed, too great to remain
Separated, sisters torn
Yet I was blessed, my fortune to attain

For the family I found, filled me with love
They nurtured, taught and showed me how to
live
Through time, their kindness, a gift from above
A second chance, a life they would give
A transformation, guided with grace
From a wounded girl to one free from strife

Fortunate, I am to have found this place
A home where love and acceptance reside
Through hardships and pain I had to face
With family, I've learned to thrive

Mount pleasant lane

On mount pleasant lane, a road of shadows
I once resided, in a complex of flats
Where the elder souls sought solace and peace
21 was the number
Yet, in what was meant to be a haven a storm
brewed silently

The foster carer, a warden of neglect
Granny Mary, a name we whispered with dread
In that desolate flat, our innocence was stripped
Abuse and torment, the life we had to live

For three long years, we languished in despair
No rescuer came, no saviour appeared
As social services turned a blind eye
Our plans for help were swallowed by the night
Then, a miracle happened my forever parents
saved me from hell

Whom shall I blame for this wretched
predicament
The culprits, they stand with their faces unseen
Social services, the guardians who failed
My birth family, a dysfunctional scene

But blame cannot heal the wounds
That lives deep within my tender heart
The scars I bear, both seen and unseen
Are reminders of a past that tore me apart
Yet in the depths of darkness, a light did shine
A strength within me begins to rise
With resilience as my armour, I forged ahead
To reclaim my life, to embrace my own skies

For I am not defined by the road we once tread
on
Nor the labels imposed upon my fragile soul
I am a warrior, survivor rising above

So let me find solace in our shared pain
In the unity of voices speaking truth
For through our stories we reclaim our worth
And pave a path for healing and resolute

Mount pleasant lane, a chapter long closed
I rise from the ashes, my spirit reclaimed
No longer a victim, but a warrior strong
In the tapestry of life, my own destinies will
appear

Beacon Lodge

In a mother and baby unit, I once did reside
An adoptee's journey, a rollercoaster ride
Eight weeks which should have been tender and
bittersweet moments
Ended up in heartache and separation

Twelve weeks was the plan, a chance to bond
and grow
But life had other plans instead, as I would soon
come to know
She was given a choice, to stay or depart
And she chose to return to the life she knew
To my birth father, who hid a shadow
And I, left behind, my heart feeling grim
My birth father more important than her own
child

Assessments on my birth father, they were never
made
His criminal record, in denial it stayed
The truth obscured, a darkness concealed
But the whispers of doubt could not be ignored
And the weight of uncertainty was deeply
revealed
A shadow cast upon our fragile thread

At eight months, the police took me away
To the foster home where I once stayed before
this home
My older sister waiting for me there
Yet longing lingers for a birth mother's embrace
Separated and lost, in a world so unknown
The foundation of my life, forever overthrown
In a world where chaos had left it's trace

Birth mother spoke of suicide, a haunting
thought
A shattered soul, burdened by despair
Leaving me to question, if love was truly there

Though the road was rough, and the path unclear
I have grown stronger, conquering my fear
The scars may linger, but the spirit will rise
For I am a survivor, with resilience in my eyes

And though the journey was filled with pain and
strife
I've learned to embrace my story, for it has
shaped my life

A grandmother's push

In the realm of secrets and shadows
A tale of anguish and pain unfolds
A story whispered in hushed tones
Of a birth mother's untold truth unknown

In the depths of her heart she carried me
A life blooming within, a bond forever
unestablished
But fate conspired with a cruel hand
Unveiling a web of darkness unplanned

At six months pregnant she stood alone
Her mother's disapproval an ominous tone
For my birth father's sins a haunting past
A tale of abuse a storm that would last

In the year of 1988 a vile act transpired
A niece's innocence, forever scarred
And as the truth emerged like a bitter tide
My birth mother's world was shattered denied

And in the depths of despair, my birth mother
fell
Pushed down the stairs, a moment where
darkness dwells

Her mother consumed by rage and despair
Unleashed her fury a will wicked snare
Down the stairs my birth mother was pushed
A desperate act, her grandchild to discard
A horrendous act in hopes that I'd be crushed
For in her heart a twisted hope would bloom
To push my birth mother down, her unborn's
tomb

The sinister intentions are heard so cold
A grandmother's darkness a story yet untold
But within this darkness a flicker of light
A destiny entwined with courage burning bright

For within the womb, a life fought to survive
Amidst the chaos, a flicker of hope did strive
Investigations unfolded, shedding light on the
truth
My birth parents abuse, a sinister tale

Amidst investigations, my sisters pain
The abuse inflicted a family stain
My sister a victim of their horrendous crimes
Landed in the hospital, where sorrow chimes
And as my birth father wasn't her father
His cruelty unleashed leaving her forever
scarred

Before my birth the world deemed me at risk
A child protection register, a bleak abyss
I too became a name on a list
The stain of my birth parents' actions a lasting
trace
Their convictions and probation a haunting truth

But I as the bearer of this painful past
Shall rise above the shadows, break free at last
For I am not defined by the sins of my kin
I am the sculptor of my own fate, from within

In the tapestry of life, I shall weave my own
thread
No longer confined by the darkness that once
spread
For in the scars that mark my journey's path
I find strength and resilience, a love that will last

So I shall rise above like a phoenix in flight
No longer defined by a history of pain
I reclaim my story, for it's mine to gain

Yet in the midst of chaos a spirit arose
A strength within, refusing to be enclosed
For in the depths of despair, a love was born
A love that would guide me through the storm

As the years passed, the truth slowly unveiled
Through reunion the darkness came to truth
My birth mother's words, heavy with regret
A tale of a past she could never forget

But within this pain I find strength anew
A resilience shaped by the past it's true
For I am more than the history I bear
A survivor, a fighter with love I share

So I let this tale be a testament to the power
Of resilience and love that towers
For in the face of darkness we find our light
And in the depths of pain we reclaim our right

To rise above to heal to rewrite our song
To embrace the truth however long
For in the heart's journey we find our worth
A testament to the strength of our birth